*The C...*

...

belongs to

_____

BN x

# EX LIBRIS
## oF the Brooks Family
### Ellis, Felix, Marjorie
### & Vivian

# THE OZONE FRIENDLY JOKE BOOK

Kim Harris
Chris Langham
Robert Lee
Richard Turner

*Illustrated by David Farris*

BEAVER BOOKS

*The authors would like to thank*
Spitting Image *for providing them with somewhere
to work.*

A Beaver Book
Published by Arrow Books Limited
20 Vauxhall Bridge Road, London SW1V 2SA
An imprint of Random Century Group

London Melbourne Sydney Auckland
Johannesburg and agencies throughout the world

First published 1990

Text © Rosemary Canter, Kim Harris, Chris Langham,
Robert Lee, Richard Turner 1990
Illustrations © Random Century Ltd 1990

Set in Century Schoolbook
by JH Graphics Ltd, Reading

Made and printed in Great Britain
by Courier International Ltd
Tiptree, Essex

ISBN 0 09 967490 4

What do you call a whale that talks too much?
*Blubbermouth.*

What's green and conquered the world?
*Alexander the Grape.*

The jokes on the previous page were written with an unleaded pencil.

What's green and prickly?
*An oversensitive gooseberry.*

How do you start a row between conservationists?
*Pour oil on troubled waters.*

What do you do with birds caught in an oil slick?
*Give them tweetment.*

How does an elephant tell off a poacher?
*Tusk, tusk!*

How do plants spread rumours?
*Through the grapevine.*

What's green, chilly and expensive?
*A cool million.*

What do you call an orange from Chernobyl?
*A melon.*

What do gardeners from Chernobyl have?
*Incredibly green fingers.*

What's got two heads, squawks and glows in the dark?
*Chicken Kiev.*

How can you tell if the planet is running out of energy?
*Check your greengages.*

How many industrialists does it take to change a light bulb?
*No dirty jokes in this book, please!*

Doctor, Doctor, if I take these green pills will I get better?
*Well, nobody I've given them to has ever come back.*

A famous surgeon went on safari to Africa. When he came back his colleagues asked him how he got on.

'It was a real drag,' he said. 'I didn't kill anything. I'd have been better off staying here in the hospital.'

CITY BOY: That farmer's a magician.
COUNTRY BOY: *Why?*
CITY BOY: He says he's just turned his cow into a field.

I've lost my monkey-eating eagle. What shall I do? *Notify the flying squad.*

Who is Tarzan's favourite singer?
*Harry Elefante.*

Where do the last surviving blue whales meet up?
*At the International Date Line.*

Help! help! the last elephant's just fallen over a cliff!
*Is he hurt?*
Don't know. He hasn't stopped falling yet.

What do you call an ecologically-minded heir to the throne?
*The Prince of Whales.*

11

What's green and indigestible?
*The inedible hulk.*

What's green and can't be rubbed out?
*The indelible hulk.*

Why did the poacher cross the road?
*Because he wanted to get to the other hide.*

One of my uncles was a tree doctor in South America but he gave it up.
*Why?*
He just didn't have the patients.

What do you call a fruit that's near extinction?
*Endangered peaches.*

What's the name of a radioactive boxer?
*Gamma Ray Leonard.*

What do you get when Margaret Thatcher stands on a chair and talks ecology?
*A tall Tory.*

What did the two birdcatchers say to the Amazonian parrot?
*Zoo's company.*

What did the two roadbuilders say to the Amazonian forest?
*Tree's a crowd.*

What do you call a colour-blind environmental group?
*Red Peace.*

What's the name of the little girl who went out saving wolves?
*Little Green Riding Hood.*

What do you call a crazy ecologist?
*Enviro-mental.*

What do you call an intoxicated elephant?
*Trunk and disorderly.*

Why was the parrot mad?
*He was out of his tree.*

Who sailed the high seas attacking whaling ships?
*Greenbeard.*

What do you call a group of rare policemen?
*Endangered P.C.'s.*

What do you call someone who kills turtles?
*A turtle idiot.*

What clicks and kills people?
*A man-eating geiger.*

A panda walks into a Wild West bar and eats an enormous meal. A baddy suddenly points a gun at him and announces, 'This town ain't big enough for both of us.' The panda draws his gun on the baddy, has a shoot-out, wins, gets up and walks out. The bartender stops him. 'Hey, panda, you haven't paid your bill.' 'Look me up in the dictionary,' replies the panda. The bartender does: PANDA – an animal who eats shoots and leaves.

Where do they make money at the North Pole?
*In glacier mints.*

What's the most disastrous football team in Britain?
*Nottingham Rain Forest.*

What's found at the North Pole and has a hole in the middle?
*A polo bear.*

Notice on the wall of a burger joint: Staff who steal the food will not be given paid sick leave.

BOY ON THE BEACH AT SELLAFIELD: Can I go for a swim, Mummy?
MOTHER: *No. It's full of radioactive waste.*
BOY: But Daddy's swimming.
MOTHER: *Yes, but he's insured.*

What joke is just as funny the second time around?
*A recycled one.*

What's brown, good for fields and rings like a bell?
*DUNG!!*

Two germs in a laboratory dish:
FIRST GERM: What are you going to give me for Christmas?
SECOND GERM: *Rabies.*

What's green, round and smells?
*Kermit's bottom.*

What does a vegetarian lion eat?
*Swedes.*

What's steaming hot and too big to put on your toast?
*A poached elephant.*

What do you call a young environmentally-conscious fashion victim?
*A green teen that's keen to be seen.*

What happened to the big game hunter?
*Something he disagreed with ate him.*

What do you call an alligator belt?
*A waist product.*

What's another name for a poacher?
*An endangering species.*

What's green and swift?
*A runner bean.*

I'm afraid we've run out of endangered species jokes.

How do greens keep in touch with the vegetable world?
*By keeping their fingers on the pulses.*

What group is most concerned about the rising level of the world's oceans?
*Short people.*

What kind of pencil do you use to write a green joke book?
*Unleaded.*

What happened when the sherbert factory exploded?
*Acid drop rain.*

What do environmentally-conscious mice study?
*Eekology*

What do you call a rain forest that's here today but gone tomorrow?
*A topical rain forest.*

What's big and grey and sings Cole Porter songs?
*Elephantz Gerald.*

What do you call vegetable activists?
*Green Peas.*

What did the carbon monoxide say to the car?
*I'm exhausted.*

What's the best way to keep a cool head in a crisis?
*Hair conditioning.*

What do you get if you cross an ostrich with a
bookie?
*A birds that lays odds.*

What do you call a rash round the top of your
trousers?
*Toxic waist.*

What do South Americans call North American
environmentalists?
*Greengoes.*

If all the natterjacks disappeared, they'd be
toadally wiped out.

What do you call an angry toad?
*Hopping mad.*

What do you call a fat and greedy poacher?
*A big game bunter.*

What does a reformed culler in Alaska get?
*A seal of approval.*

Exposure to radiation affects your short term memory. The other thing it does is affect your short term memory.

What has spots, four legs, a tail, whiskers and flies?
*A dead leopard.*

What has spots, four legs, a tail and whiskers?
*A lynx with acne.*

What do you call a potato from Sellafield?
*An unidentified frying object.*

Why is the sand wet?
*Because the seaweed.*

What do you call a reptile that tells jokes?
*A stand-up chameleon.*

What do you call a seagull with a variety act?
*An Arctic tern.*

A panda goes into a restaurant and orders some bamboo shoots. The waiter brings the food, the panda eats it and asks for the bill. The waiter brings the bill and says, 'You know, we don't get many pandas in here.' The panda says, 'At these prices I'm not surprised.'

What do you call a flying mouse that makes music by rubbing its legs together?
*A cricket bat.*

What's another name for a sewage worker?
*A bum disposal expert.*

What's the fastest creature on four legs?
*A hedgehog in a Lamborghini.*

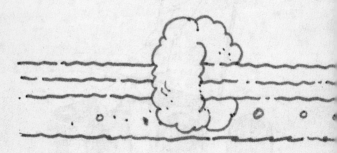

Why are geiger counters a waste of money?
*How many geigers have you seen recently?*

What are the fastest insects in the world?
*Nigel Mansell's head lice.*

What's the cleverest forest in the world?
*The Amazonian brain forest.*

What do you call an extinct vegetable?
*A hasbean.*

Who looks out for endangered vegetables?
*The Green Peas organization.*

Who was the first heroine of an ecological book?
*Anne of Green Gables.*

Where do you find an ant with a dogsled?
*Antarctica.*

Where do Italian elephants live?
*Tuscany.*

What have greedy industrialists and the Amazon jungle got in common?
*They're both dense.*

What do you call an animal that's half parrot and half tiger?
*Whatever it tells you to.*

What did the greedy industrialist do to the tree in his garden?
*Turned over a new leaf.*

What do you call an ecology-minded pop fan?
*A greenybopper.*

What is green, crisp and hard to understand?
*Lettuce think about it.*

What has bread on both sides and gets frightened easily?
*A chicken sandwich.*

What do you get when you rub two physicists together?
*Science friction.*

What's the E.E.C's biggest food mountain?
*The Trifle tower.*

What's green and round and floats in the sky?
*The Planet of the Grapes.*

What's black and hairy and surrounded by water?
*A North Sea oil wig.*

Which reptile went down the yellow brick road?
*The Lizard of Oz.*

What's got an I.Q. of 100?
*A hundred industrialists.*

Cor, she gave me a dirty look!
*Who?*
Mother Nature.

Bad news at the factory farm — all the eggs have been laid off.

A brave young ecologist said
I am going to clean up the Med
He found bikes and shoes
Several broken loos
And an Ancient Greek Sailor called Fred.

What do they sing on a factory ship?
*Whale meat again.*

What do they sing on a factory farm?
*Veal meat again.*

What has a horn, four wheels and a roof rack?
*A car?*
No, a rhino with a driving licence.

What do you call a snake in a bowler hat?
*A civil serpent.*

'I shot this magnificent beast in Africa,' said the proud hunter, standing on his lionskin rug. 'I didn't want to, it was either him or me.'

'I wonder if you would have made a better rug than him,' remarked the ecologist.

How do you stop a rhino charging?
*Take away his credit card.*

What do you call the stinking rich?
*The effluent society.*

Why did the frog order an extra drink?
*One for the toad.*

What happened to the tiger who caught the measles?
*He got so spotty, they sent him to a leopard colony.*

What lives in the jungle and is highly dangerous?
*A parrot with a machine gun.*

How do you spot a nuclear family?
*They glow in the dark.*

What rays are for adults only?
*X-rays.*

How can you spot a genetic engineer?
*It's as plain as the noses on his face.*

How do parrots put their point of view?
*They appear on squawk shows.*

Why does an ecologist wear green braces?
*To hold his trousers up.*

Why do sheep eat grass so quickly in Sellafield?
*Because two heads are better than one.*

Why did the police arrest the green beans?
*Because they were involved in a garden plot.*

Who's the most stupid man in the world?
*The global village idiot.*

Why are some jokes just as funny the third time around?
*The best jokes get recycled twice.*

What do you call a woodpecker with no beak?
*A headbanger.*

SOME BOOK TITLES:

*The Disused Railway Children*

*A Tale of Two Science Parks*

*Great Expectorations*
'That's not a green joke!
'Oh yeah? look at this hanky'

*To Not Kill a Mockingbird*

*Toad of Toad Wildlife Sanctuary*

*The Dam Builders*

Why did the three musketeers always travel with a penguin?
*Because the penguin is mightier than the sword.*

How do you spot an endangered species?
*With difficulty.*

What music do toads dance to?
*Hip hop.*

What is Robin Hood's favourite tune?
*Greensleeves.*

What's green, hairy and highly dangerous?
*David Bellamy with a machine gun.*

CONSERVATIONIST IN PET SHOP: Have you got any tigers going cheap?
ASSISTANT: *Sorry. We've only got ones that growl.*

Doctor, Doctor, I think I'm turning into a kangaroo.
*I haven't got time to waste on the likes of you. Hop it.*

PARROT IN CHEMIST SHOP: Have you got anything for chapped beaks?
CHEMIST: *How about this lip cream?*
PARROT: Thanks. I'll take it. Can you put it on my bill, please?

Who stole the sewage farm?
*The great drain robbers.*

I lost my very rare komodo dragon last week.
*Have you put an advert in the local paper yet?*
Don't be daft. He can't read.

FIRST BOY: Whales play chess, you know.
SECOND BOY: *Goodness, they must be clever.*
FIRST BOY: No, they don't win very often.

A boy walking along the road with a tiger on a lead
was stopped by a policeman: 'Are you taking that
tiger to the zoo?' he asked. 'No,' replied the boy. 'I
took him to the zoo yesterday. We're off to the
cinema today.'

What's the best way to talk to a rare 12-foot tall
man-eating bear?
*On the telephone.*

Where do baby apes sleep?
*In apricots.*

What do monsters of the deep eat?
*Fish and ships.*

Er, Dad, are you sure I'm a polar bear?
*Yes, son.*
Er, Mum, are you sure I'm a polar bear?
*Yes, son.*
Er, Dad, are you sure I'm a polar bear, not a koala
bear or a grizzly bear?
*Yes, son. You're definitely a polar bear.*
Cold for the time of year, isn't it?

Which bird is more intelligent — a chicken or a parrot?
*A parrot. Did you ever hear of Kentucky Fried Parrot?*

Why do you use a metal-coated umbrella?
*In case it acid rains.*

What joke is just as funny the fourth time around?
*The same recycled joke you saw on p. XX*

Why did the parrot wear a raincoat?
*Because he wanted to be polyunsaturated.*

When is it dangerous to go into the garden?
*When the buds are shooting.*

What do you call an underground train full of environmental experts?
*A tube of smarties.*

How do you mend a hole in a cabbage?
*Use a cabbage patch.*
How do you mend a hole in the ozone layer?
*You can't. But you can stop it growing bigger by recognising the need to look after our planet.*

How do you describe the dance of a sexy chicken?
*Poultry in motion.*

What do you call the greenhouse effect on a very small planet?
*The flowerpot effect.*

What do you need to be a cancer specialist?
*A good sense of tumour.*

What's the cure for Dutch Elm Disease?
*A tree surgeon who's good at languages.*

What form of transport is nothing but trouble?
*A bovvercraft.*

What carries 85 lorries, a load of drunken football supporters and a magic wand?
*A cross-channel fairy.*

'There is no truth in the rumour that nuclear fallout affects short term memory,' an angry spokesman said at a press conference. 'Now who are you, and what do you want?'

A fish would have to be crazy to appear in a book like this.
*It's beyond all reasonable trout.*

How to be an utterly green person:
1. Use unleaded pencils
2. Use recyled paper
3. Eat far too many sweets.

Why didn't the jellyfish cross the road?
*Because it was spineless.*

What's the ideal birthday present for a fat industrialist?
*A waist disposal unit.*

What did the sinking tanker say to the seagull?
*Oil be seeing you.*

What did the treefrog say to the stick insect?
*Stick around.*

What did the stick insect say to the treefrog?
*What on earth makes you think stick insects talk to treefrogs?*

How do you help someone who's swallowed a snail?
*Give him a slug in the mouth.*

What does Margaret Thatcher eat for breakfast?
*Greens.*

What do greens eat for breakfast?
*Margaret Thatcher.*

What's the biggest ant in the world?
*A giant.*

What adventure film is all about the search for extinct dogs?
*Raiders of the Lost Bark.*

What adventure film took place in waterproof footwear?
*Waders of the Lost Ark.*

What did Tarzan give the world's last gorilla as a parting gift?
*A comb.*

What film is all about crime in the ocean?
*The Codfather.*

What card game do crocodiles like best?
*Snap.*

What's green and stupid?
*Thick pea soup.*

Where does the leopard buy his clothes?
*Jungle sales.*

What do you call a very old worn-out bear that's
nearly extinct?
*Fred Bear.*

What do you call two spiders who just got married?
*Newlywebs.*

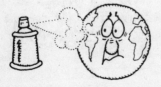

What kind of bird lives underground?
*A mynah bird.*

Why should water mammals keep quiet?
*Because they otter to be seen and not heard.*

PATIENT: I keep seeing toads in front of my eyes.
DOCTOR: *Don't worry. It's only a hoptical illusion.*

Where does a sick oil tanker go?
*To the doc.*

Which book makes bees proud?
*Lord of the Stings.*

What's green and funny on top, and yellow underneath?
*Last week's custard.*

What do you get if you cross the white of an egg with a nuclear warhead?
*A boom meringue.*

What do you call a sick bird?
*Illegal.*

What did the woman who wanted a fur coat say to the hunter?
*Don't just stand there, slay something!*

The idea that the government's policies are built on sand is totally without foundation, a Tory environment spokesman said today.

Roses are red
Violets are blue
Come acid rain,
They'll all melt in the dew.

What do you get if you cross a centipede with a parrot?
*A walkie-talkie.*

What did the gorilla say to his girlfriend?
*You drive me bananas.*

What did the vegetarian say to the butcher?
*I never want us to meat again.*

What happened when the Alaskan seal hunter was found by the Green party?
*He gave them the cold shoulder.*

What do you call a goat with a hump?
*A camel hair goat.*

What do you get if you cross a panda with a harp?
*A bear-faced lyre.*

What do you get if you cross a panda with a kangaroo?
*A fur coat with pockets.*

What's black and white and found in the desert?
*A lost panda.*

What do you get when oil tankers sink?
*Endangered beaches.*

What do you get if you cross a sheep with a kangaroo?
*A woolly jumper.*

What do you get if you cross a python with a radioactive pile?
*A twenty-foot-long striplight that can squeeze you to death.*

What do you get if you cross an octopus with a cat?
*An animal with eight legs and nine lives.*

What do you call the crows who build their nests on a nuclear power plant?
*Raven lunatics.*

What do you get if you cross a monkey with a bulldozer?
*A flat monkey.*

What do you get if you cross a leech with a parrot?
*An animal that can suck the hind legs off a donkey.*

Why are trunk calls so expensive?
*Because some stupid people have nearly made elephants extinct.*

How do you tell an elephant from an industrialist?
*An industrialist never remembers.*

Doctor, Doctor, I keep seeing elephants with green spots.
*Have you seen a psychiatrist?*
No, only elephants with green spots.

Doctor, Doctor, my elephant has swallowed a roll of film.
*Take him home, put him in a dark room and see if anything else develops.*

Why do elephants have trunks?
*Because crocodile handbags have been banned.*

Why do elephants have trunks?
*So they have somewhere to hide when they see a poacher.*

What has a trunk and four legs but can't walk?
*A dead elephant.*

What has eight legs but can't walk?
*Two dead elephants.*

What has 96 legs, 48 tusks and is blindfolded?
*A herd of elephants in front of a firing squad.*

What do you call a combination of lead, aluminium, sulphates and $H_2O$?
*Tap water.*

If this coffee tastes like mud that's because it was ground yesterday.
(Yes, I know it's not a green joke, but I'm colour blind.)

What do you get if you cross a leech with a wristwatch?
*A bloody good time.*

What do you call a very fat man trying to buy a box of Scrabble?
*A big game hunter.*

What do you call a dolphin in a flowerpot?
*A dolphinium.*

What do you call a winkle who's got protection from the mob?
*A gangster's mollusc.*

What do you call a bloke covered in shellfish?
*A musselman*

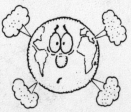

Why did the octopus take on a second job?
*He had a wife and three squids to support.*

What do you call a man in a Cortina at the bottom of the Atlantic?
*A deep sea driver.*

Why did the dolphin swim alone?
*Because he was expelled from school.*

Why aren't whales in the North Sea taken seriously?
*Because they keep spouting rubbish.*

What do you grow in a radioactive field?
*Nuclear plants.*

What happened to the greedy industrialist who had a brain transplant?
*The brain rejected him.*

Why did the elephant poacher spend two weeks in a revolving door?
*Because he couldn't find the door handle.*

What's green with checked trousers?
*Rupert the snooker table.*

If you ever need a heart transplant and you can choose between two donors: a 23-year-old marathon runner, or a 56-year-old industrialist, which would you choose?
*The industrialist's. Because you'd want a heart that had never been used.*

What's the definition of a dope ring?
*Ten whalers in a circle.*

What do you call a crazy kangaroo?
*Hopping mad.*

What's the best use for sealskin?
*To keep seals in.*

What's green and wrinkly?
*A pea that's past its sell-by date.*

What's thick and sticky and swears at seagulls?
*Crude oil.*

What shoots down Canadian rivers and then tells
you all about it?
*A travel-log.*

What do you call an ape with no legs?
*An eye-level gorilla.*

What do you say to a limpet covered in oil?
*Bye – valve!*

There were two fish in a tank. One said to the other, 'Do you know how to drive this thing?'

What do you call a peach that is green and skinny at harvest time?
*A failure.*

What is rhubarb?
*Celery with high blood pressure.*

What's green with red spots?
*A frog with measles.*

What does a brontosaurus put in his car?
*Fossil fuel.*

What jumps up and down in your custard?
*Kangarhubarb.*

What do you call a marsupial's dad?
*Parsupial.*

Why did the man from Brazil join the forestry commission?
*Because his wife told him to go to blazes.*

What do you harvest from polluted fields?
*Acid grain.*

The elephant was shot three times.
*Was it serious?*
Well, the first bullet proved fatal, but the second
two weren't too bad.

He's got a good head — for an industrialist.
*Good as new — never been used!*

What do you get if you drop a nuclear device on
a herd of cattle?
*Steak and mushroom cloud.*

75

'Ooh, I do wish this tummy ache would go away,' thought the squid as he swam slowly through the murky depths of the ocean. Just then he was spotted by a shark, who swept him up in his jaws as he swam past. 'Oh well,' muttered the squid, 'not my lucky day, I guess.' The shark stopped next to another shark.

'Hi, Fred,' he said, 'How's fins?'

'Fins ain't what they used to be,' replied the other shark.

'Cheer up!' said the first shark. 'By the way, here's that sick squid I owe you.'

What do you call a mollusc with a machine gun? *Clambo.*

# ALL THAT GLITTERS is PROBABLY RADIOACTIVE

What do you call a crustacean gangster?
*Al Caprawn.*

What do you call a very fast mollusc?
*Steve Clam.*

What do you call an inebriated Greek ecologist?
*Ouzo friendly.*

Roses are black
Violets are red
*What was that explosion in the night?*

When do you put stoats in your fuel tank?
*When you run out of weasel fuel.*

Little Miss Muffet
Sat on her tuffett
Ate tuna and died in a minute,
Along came a spider who sat down beside her and
said
'It's the mercury in it.'

Little Jack Horner
Got sick in his corner
From salmon and thereupon fainted.
The spider inspected
The brand Jack selected
and said, 'Seems like everything's tainted.'

Famous last words:
How do we know Julius Caesar died of mercury
poisoning?
*His last words were, 'Ate tuna, Brute.'*